SANTA FE
Dancing Ground of the Sun

Photography by Bill Bonebrake
Text by Lorraine S. Bonebrake

New Mexico Littlebooks

WESTCLIFFE PUBLISHERS
www.westcliffepublishers.com

DEDICATION
For all who supported us along our journey.

International Standard Book Number: 1-56579-239-4
Photographs © Bill Bonebrake, 1997. All rights reserved.
Text © Lorraine S. Bonebrake, 1997. All rights reserved.

Publisher's Cataloging-in-Publication:

Bonebrake, Bill.
    Santa Fe, dancing ground of the sun / Bill Bonebrake,
Lorraine S. Bonebrake.
        p. cm. — (New Mexico littlebooks ; 1)
        ISBN: 1-56579-239-4

        1. Santa Fe (N.M.)—Pictorial works. 2. Santa Fe (N.M.)—
Guidebooks.   I. Bonebrake, Lorraine S. II. Title.

F804.S243B66 1997   978.9'56
                                           QBI97-40448

Editor: Jody Berman   Production Manager: Harlene Finn
Designer: Amy Bransfield

Published by:
Westcliffe Publishers, Inc., P.O. Box 1261
Englewood, Colorado 80150
www.westcliffepubishers.com
Printed in Hong Kong by C&C Offset Printing Co., Ltd.

First frontispiece: Cathedral of St. Francis of Assisi at sunset
Second frontispiece: Wheeler Peak, Sangre de Cristo Mountains
Third frontispiece: Buttressed adobe church at sunset with rainbow
Opposite: Clay suns

For more information about other fine books and calendars from Westcliffe Publishers,
please contact your local bookstore, call us at 1-800-523-3692, write for our free
color catalog, or visit us on the Web at **www.westcliffepublishers.com**.

PREFACE

The magical character of the Southwest is defined by many elements. Among the most remarkable of these is the sun. In New Mexico the sun's rays bathe the high desert landscape in a warm splendor, unforgettable to anyone who visits here. The light is at times soft and muted, at other times intense and dramatic, providing an ever-changing palette.

Light in the Southwest is dynamic, and its quality is unparalleled. In Santa Fe one encounters light cascading over adobe walls, spilling through doorways, sparkling on water, glistening on snow, saturating color. Perhaps the most beautiful light is created at dawn and then again at dusk. The cherry-red glow of a New Mexico sunset is breathtaking. The Sangre de Cristo Mountains were named "Blood of Christ" by the conquistadors who witnessed the marvelous effect of the setting sun on their peaks.

Throughout the history of New Mexico's Indian cultures, the sun has played a significant role. In the Pueblo religion it is revered as Father Sun. The Pueblo people are his children, "a people who live on the roof of the world," and to whom the sun is vital.

The sun provides sustenance in various ways. It enables crops such as corn, beans, and squash to grow and produce food. It bakes the earth into mud layers, building walls for shelter, and it melts the snows in the mountains, sending down precious water to drink and irrigate fields.

Thus, each day Pueblo Indians pray to the sun, helping their father to move across the sky. Should they cease their prayers, they believe that the sun will no longer rise and night will descend forever over the world. What a tragedy should the light leave New Mexico and the sun cease to move across its land.

My first visit to New Mexico and Santa Fe was as a young boy. Not surprisingly, I was more interested in cowboys and Indians at the time than in the quality of light and subject matter the region offers to artists and photographers. But I do remember the strong impression that it made on me and knew that I wanted to return someday.

In 1990 I moved to Santa Fe with my wife, and

Stepped adobe wall and door

it was here that we established our first home. The sheer beauty and romance of the area caused us to choose Santa Fe over any other place in the world to begin our journey together. Its gentle, intimate, natural environment coupled with a strong cultural atmosphere offered the perfect combination for our interests in life.

I did not go to Santa Fe as a professional photographer, although for many years prior, my camera had been a constant companion, enabling me to record my adventures on film. I had traveled throughout Europe, completed a yearlong trip around the world, and lived in Germany for two years before moving to Santa Fe. In each of these places, I used my camera to translate my experiences to a visual medium, working to capture their essence.

Santa Fe changed my life significantly. I was captured by its spell. Photographing its many subjects and moods was irresistible. Its light, shapes, and colors were as unique as other magnificent places I had been to such as the Seychelles and Nepal. But in Santa Fe one experiences a heightening of the senses, a renewed awareness. I began to pursue photography the way an artist works with a canvas. I found satisfaction in shape, form, and composition, enjoying subtleties of color and shade, and loving the discipline involved with the uncertainty of changing light.

Thus, it was in Santa Fe that I became a devoted photographer. This is due as much to the people as to the place. Few places in the world are as unconditionally supportive of the "dubiously talented." In Santa Fe I began to show my work publicly and received enthusiastic support. This excitement continues today and inspires me to reach new heights in my craft.

It is a privilege for me to present this book of photography on Santa Fe and its surrounding areas. Capturing the beauty here, in this "dancing ground of the sun," as Pueblo legend calls it, offers limitless possibilities to a photographer. I am not alone in my love for this wondrous place. Many others have come before me seeking inspiration, and many will follow. Santa Fe's fragile, fleeting beauty nurtures the creative spirit and soothes the soul; yet, it does not keep you. I can only hope to give back to Santa Fe what it has given me, enriching my life.

— Bill Bonebrake

Christmas Eve at Nedra Matteucci's Fenn Gallery

The magnificent city of Santa Fe is nestled at the foot of the Sangre de Cristo Mountains. It lies in the midst of the stunning Rio Grande valley, cradle to civilizations and cultures old and new. For centuries this magical place has attracted a variety of people, each in search of a different promise.

Seeking fertile land, ancient people settled in the sun-drenched tranquillity between the mountains, built earthen structures, and formed communities. Their descendants, the Pueblo people, flourished and multiplied. Spanish conquistadors disrupted this culture in search of gold and with the aim of spreading Christianity throughout this new, untamed world. Next, frontiersmen penetrated the land, seeking adventure, building settlements, and establishing valuable trade routes. More recently, artists, writers, and soul seekers have sought out Santa Fe for its rich cultural heritage, inspiring landscape, and nurturing spirit.

Pueblo Bonito, Chaco Culture National Historic Park

Rio Chama, tributary of the Rio Grande

Ancient Peoples

Even before people rested their eyes on New Mexico, it was a land of startling beauty. The area in which Santa Fe lies was one of great volcanic activity that resulted in the formation of dramatic mountain ranges and gorges that surround Santa Fe today.

The Jemez Mountains rise to the west, and the Sangre de Cristos to the east. To the north lie the Rio Grande rift and the plateau on which Taos perches in the shadow of Wheeler Peak, New Mexico's highest point, at 13,161 feet. From this northern plateau descends the Rio Grande River, winding its way through narrow canyons and across fertile valleys, bringing rich volcanic silt to the area's future residents. The red earth, so commonly recognized as customary of New Mexico, results from the oxidation of iron present in the igneous rock that makes up much of the region's terrain.

Lava flow, El Malpais National Monument

Chimney Rock at the Ghost Ranch, Abiquiu

The first people most likely to have entered the present-day Santa Fe area were Asiatic migrants who crossed the northern land bridge 12,000 to 15,000 years ago and traveled slowly southward. They were hunters and gatherers whose nomadic lifestyle made them rugged, primitive peoples. Gradually, over thousands of years, these nomads began to utilize the natural resources of the land more efficiently. And as the last continental glaciers retreated further to the north, the region became warmer, more arid, and the people remained.

Pueblo Bonito, Chaco Culture National Historic Park

It was only natural that these people should seek out a fertile river basin such as the Rio Grande and its many tributaries such as the Santa Fe River. By the first century, with the introduction of cultural innovations from the south, namely agriculture, stonemasonry, textiles, and an evolving cooperative social system, these once nomadic tribes settled into communities. Such communities formed throughout

Aztec Ruins National Monument

Jeméz State Monument

Bandelier National Monument

northern New Mexico, and the inhabitants came to be known as the Anasazi, loosely translated as "ancient ones."

Although only remnants of the Anasazi remain, the ruins of their culture are quite revealing. The Anasazi, an agrarian people, constructed their dwellings along the sides of cliffs overlooking their crops, or on flatter lands close to water. They used stones to construct the walls of their shelters and pine logs to support the roofs. Some Anasazi also lived in cave dwellings.

Anasazi communities developed into multi-storied "apartment houses," some, such as the ones in Chaco Canyon, housing up to 5,000 people. Smaller settlements such as Bandelier had as many as 400 rooms. The Anasazi used sacred kivas, circular chambers built below ground, to conduct religious ceremonies and social meetings. Their culture flourished until about 1250 when a disaster—what most believe to be severe drought—caused them to abandon their settlements and move closer to the water's mother source, the Rio Grande.

The Anasazi merged with other groups in this region, and evolved into the current Pueblo culture. The Pueblo trace their ancestry through "emergence myths," believing that they rose from the earth's womb, migrated over countless centuries, until settling at their present sites. The Indians of San Ildefonso Pueblo,

Petroglyph National Monument

about twenty miles northwest of Santa Fe, consider Bandelier to have been one of the many stops along the migratory path to their present home.

Although there is evidence that at first this melding and settling of communities was not always peaceful, as recorded in the area's ancient petroglyphs, in time the Pueblo Indians came to prosper in their new homes, building on many traditions and practices of their rich ancestry. This is best represented in their manner of communal living and multistoried buildings.

Whereas the Anasazi built with stone, the Pueblo people utilized mud, dribbled

Taos Pueblo

and smoothed on a surface, layer by layer, to build walls. This technique is known as puddling. Pine logs, now called vigas, served as roof supports. As the Anasazi had done, the Pueblo Indians made use of ladders to access their homes. The ceremonial kiva was retained and is still used as a religious, cultural, and social center. Traditions of pottery also continue in their increasingly intricate designs. Well-known potters of today often come from long lines of artistic families, and distinct styles are associated with specific pueblos.

Of the eight northern pueblos stretching between Santa Fe and Taos, the Taos Pueblo is the most picturesque and well preserved. The beautifully tiered adobe structure rises five stories. The pueblo was founded around 1300, but the construction we see today dates mostly from after the Pueblo Rebellion of 1680. The main structure is no longer inhabited, however, Taosenos still utilize the lower levels to sell their handmade art and crafts. Visitors can also enjoy hot bread baked in the traditional manner in outdoor adobe beehive ovens.

Pueblo pot on stepped adobe wall

European Conquest

The relatively tranquil lifestyle the Pueblo people had come to know by the early 1500s was about to be shattered as rumors of glittering cities of gold north of Mexico captured the imaginations of ambitious Spaniards. The medieval legend of the Seven Cities of Cibola perplexed and excited the Spanish who had ventured to the New World. The fabled stories gained strength as Aztec and Inca cities were plundered further south, yielding numerous treasures.

Determined to claim vast riches, Don Francisco Vasquez de Coronado led the first party of Europeans into present-day New Mexico in 1540. Little did these proud con-

quistadors know that the cities of gold they would encounter would be made of dirt. The radiant New Mexico sun may have bathed the adobe walls and winding paths in a golden glow, but this was not the treasure the Spaniards were seeking.

Frustrated but resolute, the conquistadors would eventually claim this resplendent land for Spain. In 1598 Don Juan de Oñate led the first great colonizing expedition into the Rio Grande valley. This first attempt failed, but in the winter of 1609–1610 Don Pedro de Peralta successfully established a settlement, making Santa Fe its capital.

Flowering yucca, state flower of New Mexico

Pueblo Bonito, Chaco Culture National Historic Park

Overleaf: View of Santa Fe

San Geronimo Chapel, Taos Pueblo

The marks made by the Spanish occupation are indelible, and evidence of their presence abounds in Santa Fe today. The Plaza, modeled after the Spanish "plaza mayor," or main square, remains at the heart of the city and its public activities. Over the span of nearly 400 years, the grounds of the Plaza have witnessed Pueblo rebellions, the most successful in 1680, the raising of the Mexican flag in 1821, and

Palace of the Governors

the subsequent raising of the Stars and Stripes in 1846. It stood at the end of the Santa Fe Trail, and today, every August, it hosts the largest Indian Arts Market in the world. The Plaza remains a crossroads and gathering place for locals and visitors alike from countries spanning the globe.

On the north side of the Plaza is the Palace of the Governors, a long, low, fortresslike complex built in 1610. Four flags have flown over the palace, which has served as a governmental seat for Spain, Mexico, the Confederate States, and the United States. The structure still stands today as the oldest continuously used public building

The Plaza

in the United States and is now a museum where visitors may visually experience the essence of Spanish colonial life. Outside, under the palace's portal and facing the Plaza, Native American artisans sell their wares just as they have for hundreds of years on the same spot.

The "Oldest House"

When the Spanish entered New Mexico, they sought out not only gold and land but also souls to convert to Christianity. Santa Fe's original name, La Villa Real de la Santa Fe—the Royal City of the Holy Faith—is indicative of the central concerns of the Spaniards, namely their king and their God. Today the bell towers, turrets, spires, and crosses erected by the Spanish rise amidst the squat adobe structures, puncturing the cobalt blue sky.

The marriage of traditional adobe and the Spanish Mission style is beautiful to behold in structures such as the Chapel of San Miguel, built in 1626 and rebuilt in 1710, and the Santuario de Guadalupe, erected in 1795. Additional examples of Spanish Mission style adobe churches may be seen further north in Chimayo, Ranchos de Taos, and at the Taos Pueblo.

El Santuario de Chimayó

$\int$anta Fe gracefully incorporates other styles of churches as well. Loretto Chapel, also known as Our Lady of Light Chapel, exemplifies the Gothic Revival style and was designed and constructed between 1874 and 1878 by French architect Projectus Mouly. Its alter was made in Italy, and the chapel features an expertly crafted spiral staircase—constructed without nails or visible support—whose builder remains a mystery.

The Cathedral of St. Francis of Assisi, one of Santa Fe's most imposing structures, represents the Romanesque style. Built under the auspices of Archbishop J. B. Lamy, its style was native to Lamy's Auvergne, France, making it foreign to Santa Fe's Spanish heritage and Indian background. It was designed by Antoine Mouly and his son, Projectus, but it took many years to complete under several architects. Begun in 1869, it wasn't consecrated until 1886.

The details of domestic and commercial architecture that are so readily associated with Santa Fe and its world-famous style find their roots in Spanish influences and innovations. The Spanish Pueblo style incorporates the use of sun-baked adobe bricks, an important development in building with adobe. In

Spiral staircase, Loretto Chapel

Loretto Chapel

Overleaf: White cross on stepped adobe wall

domestic architecture, inner court-
yards, or patios, were widely used as
were interior chimneyed fireplaces,
usually situated in a corner. The surrounding of open spaces with portals,
or porches, became widespread in both
commercial and domestic design, and
the addition of elaborately carved ceil-
ing beams, capitals, and bolsters con-
tributed to the style's charm. Decorative
wooden gates and doors set into long

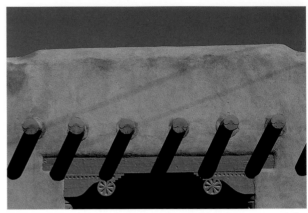

Rosette-carved corbels and vigas on adobe

adobe walls became the hallmark of Spanish Pueblo style and the Santa Fe style of today.

Such picturesque remnants of Santa Fe's Spanish past endure along the Acequia
Madre, or Mother Ditch, which itself is a significant part of the city's colonial history. In
settling Santa Fe, the Spanish introduced their system of irrigation and engineered ditches
to transport vital water to the city. Over 300 years later the Acequia Madre still flows,
nourishing fruit trees that border its sides.

Over the centuries, homes were built along the winding, shady acequia, many
exhibiting features typical of Spanish Pueblo style. Among the earliest was a farmhouse,
consisting of six rooms, with a portal, an enclosed placita, and a corral. Adobe walls still
surround such compounds, and homes are accessed through heavy wooden or iron gates
and doors that are reached by crossing over bridges spanning the narrow ditch. Features
that today offer privacy and charm once provided protection from hostile assaults.

Adobe residence

Spring blossoms on Acequia Madre

Sunset over Santa Fe

Peace rose

American Southwest

The period of Spanish rule was one of utter isolation: Trade was permitted only with Mexico, and the Chihuahua Trail, which stretched between Chihuahua and Santa Fe, was the only link to the outside world. At the close of the eighteenth century, however, the situation began to change. The Louisiana Purchase in 1803 opened up the American West, and adventurers such as Zebulon Pike penetrated Spain's territory. In 1821 Mexico won its independence from Spain, and the dark curtain was lifted.

Mexico encouraged trade with the United States, and the 800-mile Santa Fe Trail was immediately blazed from Independence, Missouri. The trail ended at the Plaza, where 100 years later La Fonda Hotel was built to house travelers. Newcomers marveled at the burgeoning Southwestern city. America's fascination with Santa Fe would be continuous.

The opening of the Santa Fe Trail in 1822, with the influx of traders, trappers, merchants, ranchers, and their goods, brought a prosperous economy to the region. The effect on Santa Fe was clearly

Sunflower and cosmos

Casa Benavides Bed and Breakfast Inn, a former nineteenth century Indian trading post, Taos.

evidenced by the emergence of trading posts. Indian arts and crafts gained wide exposure and became a valuable and sought-after commodity. Also, an endless list of new provisions poured into the city.

Navajo Eyedazzler

Once again the face of Santa Fe would be forever altered. Mill-made windows with double-hung sash replaced handmade ones, allowing New Mexicans to enjoy cool breezes in their homes. New tools, hardware, and supplies encouraged innovative architectural designs and details. White-painted woodwork was a popular choice, and slender, rectangular columns replaced heavy ornate poles.

New building practices added durability to the otherwise fragile adobe walls and assisted in the preservation of historic homes and sites. Hard-burned bricks became widely used to protect exposed adobe parapets. This practical and decorative feature became symbolic of Santa Fe's Territorial style. Even more significant, the practice of covering traditional adobe walls with lime and later cement stucco, served to preserve structures that may not have endured otherwise.

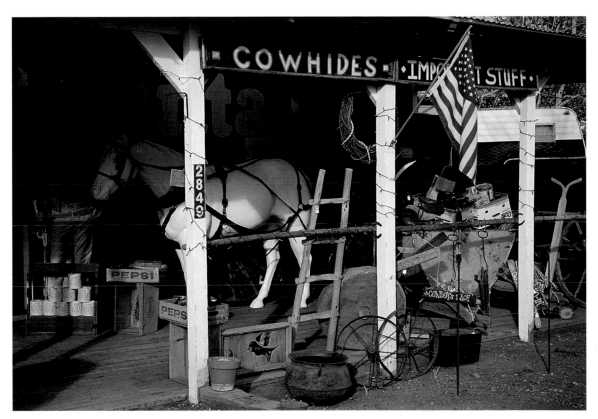

Trading post, Madrid

While the Santa Fe Trail opened the city to the Midwest, in 1879 the coming of the railroad opened Santa Fe to the East. Stories of New Mexico's beauty attracted artists, writers, businessmen, and those wanting to improve their health. These people did not seek adventure as much as they sought solace and a place to establish residency. Many of these individuals were instrumental in preserving Santa Fe's architectural landmarks.

Dr. Edgar Lee Hewett, founding director of the Museum of New Mexico, came to Santa Fe from the East as a scholarly entrepreneur and an accomplished archaeologist. His pioneering vision and determination established Santa Fe as an alluring and exciting ground for artists. With the support of his friend and colleague, Robert Henri, who then recruited George Bellows and Leon Kroll—all three prominent artists working in America—Hewett successfully exhibited modern art in New Mexico with an excitement akin to that generated by more established museums such as the Carnegie Museum in Pittsburgh and the Chicago Art Institute. Hewitt also saved the Palace of the Governors from deterioration as well as its many historic treasures by overseeing the building's restoration and establishing it as a museum.

Camino del Monte Sol

Adobe abstract

*I*n the late 1920s Santa Feans such as Margretta S. Dietrich helped preserve Santa Fe's past by purchasing and restoring private residences in danger of demolition. In 1927 she bought El Zaguan, now considered one of New Mexico's most important buildings. Once the home of a prominent merchant during the days of the Santa Fe Trail, El Zaguan boasts a long covered corridor that extends from an open

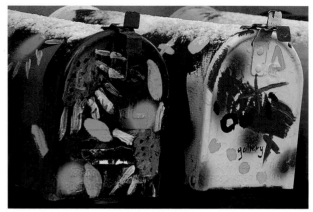

One-of-a-kind mailboxes, Bottler Dane Gallery

patio at the east to a large garden at the west. Rooms designed in the Territorial style were later added to the original two- or three-roomed adobe home, stretching El Zaguan for 300 feet along lower Canyon Road.

With the influx of new residents interested in the arts and Santa Fe's unique place in history, the city's first artists' colony was formed in 1921. Its original members shared a fascination with the New Mexico landscape and called themselves, simply, Los Cinco Pintores, or the Five Painters. Jozef Bakos, Fremont Ellis, Walter Mruk, Willard Nash, and Will Shuster quickly gained reputations as eccentrics, choosing to live and work in residences and studios built in the traditional adobe style. They were good-naturedly dubbed "the five nuts in five mud huts" by fellow Santa Feans.

Canyon Road galleries and studios

Overleaf: Hand-crafted bell and farolitos

*C*amino del Monte Sol was their chosen street of residence, and even today homes strung along this "Way of the Mountain Sun," climbing gracefully up to the sky, don artistic decorations such as chili ristras on the doors.

The Five Painters' studios were located nearby, along Canyon Road, a picturesque, winding trail that had once been an Indian footpath leading over the Sangre de Cristos to Pecos Pueblo. Canyon Road, despite its well-known and highly publicized reputation for its world-class galleries, still has an intimacy about it. Its seemingly unbroken string of adobes, gardens, and walls hug its dusty sides. The galleries housed in these simple, low structures exhibit fine arts and crafts spanning thousands of years and hundreds of cultures.

Perhaps the Five Painters succeeded in their goal to "bring art to the people," for Canyon Road provides an opportunity for visitors to leisurely stroll its narrow walks and explore its hidden alleyways with wonder. On Canyon Road artist studios are still in use and unknown talent is tirelessly sought. Native American pottery, old and new, is seen displayed alongside contemporary American paintings. Jewelry, sculpture,

Wreath on blue door

quilts, hand-loomed textiles, and other one-of-a-kind creations are also exhibited in the fine galleries.

Christmas Eve, Jane Smith Gallery, Canyon Road

The welcoming spirit of Canyon Road is best expressed on Christmas Eve when its merchants, artists, and residents line the street with bonfires and farolitos—glowing candles set in brown bags. No surface is left unadorned. The farolitos also line walls, paths, roofs, and alleys, creating a magnificent pattern of flickering light. Carolers gather around the bonfires often accompanied by a guitar or a trumpet. Everyone is welcome to participate as the joyous procession slowly moves up the road.

Throughout Santa Fe, Christmastime is enchanting. Residents and businesses adorn their "City of the Holy Faith" with traditional decorations that, while seemingly commonplace in other locales, take on an exquisite Southwestern charm. A wreath set against a blue door, an adobe wall, or a lace curtain captures the festive mood. A snowfall in Santa Fe can be spellbinding, as walls, ladders, and gates are outlined in a powdery white.

Favorite Places

Santa Fe tantalizes the senses and stimulates the imagination. Attractions from museums to galleries, restaurants to shops, hotels to spas, and opera to skiing are gems on the surface of a rich history. In experiencing Santa Fe's many features, past merges harmoniously with present and makes the visit extraordinary.

When selecting accommodations in Santa Fe, one may choose to lodge at the end of the Santa Fe Trail at La Fonda Hotel where notable characters such as Kit Carson spent the night and Billy the Kid is said to have washed dishes. In the evening, the sound of flamenco guitars loft through the lobby; by day, light pours into a central courtyard used for dining, making for a truly memorable occasion.

A traveler may decide to repose at the Inn at Loretto. Designed in the Pueblo Revival style, this multitiered adobe structure is adjacent to the Loretto Chapel and served as a Catholic girls' school in the nineteenth century under Archbishop Lamy's direction.

The intimate and fashionable Inn of the Anasazi, named in celebration of the "enduring and creative spirit" of ancient people of New Mexico, pays tribute to the past while venerating the present. Both its exterior and interior design reflect all aspects of contemporary Santa Fe style at its best.

Dining in Santa Fe is an experience unto itself. Not only is the cuisine outstanding and innovative, the atmospheres in which one may dine are numerous. Consider sampling some of Santa Fe's most creative contemporary Southwestern dishes at Geronimo's. Located on Canyon Road, Geronimo's was once the residence

Ristras on Inn at Loretto

Inn of the Anasazi

of a soldier who served in the eighteenth century Spanish army.

Or try Santacafe, known for its modern American fare with a Southwestern and Asian twist. Santacafe is set in the former home of Padre Gallegos, a controversial nineteenth-century priest who is believed to have helped organize an attempted revolt against the Americans in 1846.

Chili ristras

One may wish to sample New Mexican cuisine with a continental flair at La Casa Sena. The Territorial style home, built in 1867 by Civil War hero Major José Sena, overlooks a stunning courtyard.

Nearby, the Shed offers some of the best traditional Hispanic pueblo cooking in Santa Fe. Tucked away in a rambling hacienda with a playful, mazelike interior, the Shed has old wooden floors, low doors, and whimsically painted walls. In 1693 the property on which the Shed sits was awarded to a conquistador named Diego Arias de Quiros for his brave role in the reconquest of New Spain under General de Vargas.

A visitor may linger on the second-story balcony of the Ore House on the Plaza, savoring fresh seafood and hardy steaks. Here, one can enjoy a sweeping view of historic Santa Fe, including the Plaza, St. Francis Cathedral, and the end of the Santa Fe Trail, all set against the majestic Sangre de Cristo Mountains.

Cart of chili ristras

To explore the relics of Santa Fe's rich past, tourists may choose from an excellent selection of museums. Santa Fe's oldest museum, the Museum of New Mexico, was established in 1908 and today consists of four separate museums.

The Palace of the Governors, located on the Plaza, is a historic landmark, and reflects the history of New Mexico and its varied cultures.

In addition to honoring its past, Santa Fe has always supported its contemporary arts. Thus, in 1917, the Museum of New Mexico was expanded to include the Museum of Fine Arts. The director, Dr. Edgar Lee Hewett, wanted to exhibit the works of New Mexico artists of the period, whether "eminent painter or sculptor, unknown beginner, or humblest of Indian, all on equal terms." This spirit of openness continues today. While housing modern works, the Museum of Fine Arts pays tribute to the region's past through its architecture and interior design. The building, designed by I. H. Rapp and William M. Rapp, represents the Pueblo Revival style and incorporates elements from the facades of mission churches in Acoma, Laguna, and San Felipe pueblos. The interior furnishings, doors, and large

The Frank Howell Gallery

The Museum of Fine Arts

carved vigas reflect the Spanish Colonial Revival style. Attractively patterned chairs, tables, chests, and sideboards grace the museum's rooms and halls.

The Museum of Indian Arts and Culture, established in 1987, again successfully blends past with present. The visitor is catapulted back in time when viewing eleventh-century Anasazi pottery. The museum also features the work of present-day Pueblo and Navajo potters as well as some Anglo artists working in the ancient tradition.

The newest museum, the Museum of International Folk Art, contains roughly 120,000 objects of historic and contemporary folk art from around the world. The impressive collection includes weavings, miniature villages, wood carvings, tin works, and other items honoring the state's Hispanic art traditions.

Santa Fe's commitment to its heritage and support of its contemporary art culture are further evidenced in the items offered in private galleries and shops throughout the city. Visitors, whether professional collector or souvenir shopper, will find endless choices of unusual purchases.

The Original Trading Post on San Francisco Street is a testament to the durability of Santa Fe's

Wheeler Peak, Sangre de Cristo Mountains

history of commerce. It is believed that a tent of mesquite poles and hides was initially erected on this site as early as 1603. The present building, rustic and unique in its appearance, is over 200 years old and dates back to the Territorial style. Catering over the centuries to Indians, Spaniards, and Anglos, The Original Trading Post offered drums, moccasins, blankets, pots, baskets, bows and arrows, bead-

The Original Trading Post

work, guns, and jewelry, as well as ancient Indian and Spanish artifacts. These items were displayed in a large courtyard. Burros in nearby stalls carried the goods through Burro Alley and over long, dusty trails to Mexico and to the United States. The list of goods for sale today has grown, and the clientele now spans the globe.

Strolling under the portals of Palace Avenue and San Francisco Street, shoppers can find treasures from the region as well as from all over the world. The jewelry, textiles, and furniture of local artisans are featured in many stores, and there is no shortage of Santa Fe's quintessential souvenirs such as chili ristras and bleached skulls. Yet Santa Fe also incorporates decorative works from many foreign cultures into its unique style. Architectural pieces and ornaments such as richly carved doors, columns, and windows from India; kilims from Pakistan, Turkey, Afghanistan, India, and Russia; tiles from Mexico; and basketry from Africa all meld beautifully and add to Santa Fe's distinct charm.

Santa Fe and its marvelous tapestry of history—past and present—is a vital part of world culture. In these rapidly changing times, few places remain where history may be experienced in so intimate and immediate a setting. But in Santa Fe a timeless quality persists, and it goes much further than successfully preserving objects behind glass. At any given moment, one may still experience the same sensations known by earlier inhabitants—be they Anasazi, Pueblo, Spanish, Mexican, or American.

The distinctive, sweet scent of burning piñon still lingers in the air. The flavor of corn, beans, and chilies define the cuisine. The relaxing warmth that radiates from a sun-drenched adobe wall, as one rests against it, soothes the soul. And the whisper of a gentle breeze or a gliding snowfall quiets a busy mind. To the eye, Santa Fe remains true to its past and intoxicates us with its present beauty. Whether viewing an ancient ruin, a pueblo structure, a Spanish church, a settler's home, or a modern residence, the rich glow of adobe endures.

Skulls on blue wall, Featherston Trading Company, Ranchos de Taos